Shotokan Karate
KATA
Volume 2

Joachim Grupp

SHOTOKAN KARATE

KATA
VOLUME 2

Meyer & Meyer Sport

Original title: Shotokan Karate
Kata Band 2
Aachen, Meyer und Meyer 2003
Translated by James Beachus
Proof-reading: Suzanne Genery

British Library Cataloguing in Publication Data
A catalogue for this book is available from the British Library

Joachim Grupp:
Shotokan Karate Kata Vol.2
– Oxford: Meyer und Meyer, (UK) Ltd., 2003
ISBN 1-84126-091-6

Aachen, Adelaide, Auckland, Budapest, Graz, Johannesburg,
Miami, Olten (CH), Oxford, Singapore, Toronto
Member of the World
Sports Publishers' Association
www.w-s-p-a.org

Printed and bound by Finidr – s. r. o. Vimperk
ISBN 1-84126-091-6
E-Mail: verlag@m-m-sports.com
www.m-m-sports.com

Index

Foreword

Every reader of this book should already know something about basic Shotokan Kata. They form part of the basics that should be mastered before you start with a study of the Kata contained here. In my book "Shotokan Karate – Kata Volume 1", you'll find the basic Kata for the Shotokan style together with numerous tips and examples of their application.

"Shotokan Karate – Kata Volume 2" builds on Volume 1 and aims at readers, who are familiar with the basic Kata as well as the principle basics of the techniques. In other words aiming at Karateka, who have already spent many hours training. This book brings the whole spectrum of the 26 Shotokan Kata to completion.

Therefore, an extensive explanation of the basic terminology and techniques in Karate, the historic traditions of Shotokan Karate and the training methods can all be dispensed with. Interested, advanced Karateka will find these in my book "Shotokan Karate – Kihon, Kumite, Kata" (Oxford, 2002) and "Shotokan Karate – Kata Volume 1" (Oxford, 2003).

At this juncture I would like to include a short summary of the most important points that should be noted when training and practising the Kata forms.

Why do we practise the Kata? What are Kata? What was behind this book? Kata, the laid down, traditional form of techniques used against more than one attackers, are the essential elements of Karate. All today's elements of Karate stem from the Kata. In order to master them, it demands a preparedness to practice endlessly and a requirement to delve intensively into the details of each of them.

For those prepared to undertake this task, it is guaranteed that they will gain a tremendous experience, which transcends well over the simple execution of each of the techniques. It is not a question of a few hours or several weeks of training. One should not kid oneself with the illusion that a Kata can be mastered in a short time. Those seeking a quick success should turn their interest to another discipline. Many years are needed in order to master the demanding repertoire of movements and the numerous possibilities of using them.

The fascination of the Kata opens the way for everyone, who has sufficient patience, to endlessly practice their techniques and sequences and continually improve their execution. This book should contribute to support these aims and assist the Karateka to perfect his prowess in the Kata, whether it is in order to pass grading tests or be used in routine training, or, just simply a work-up of Karate-Do for competition. In respect of this, the book can help in at least one way. It can be used to complement the training in the Dojo or club, but cannot replace it. Correct breathing, tensioning the muscles and relaxing them, the interchange between rapid and slow movements, timing and many other aspects can only be learned by years of training.

I suggest Kata is not just exhausting training. Its richness springs not only from the numerous techniques, which are seldom or not at all practised in Kumite or basic training. There are techniques for close combat, grips or sequences to start throws, defence against armed aggressors, attacks against sensitive body spots, which would not be possible without danger in training with a partner – the palette of techniques contained in the Kata is almost inexhaustible. The contribution made by the Kata towards the perfection of the Karateka's ability should not be underestimated. Effort taken in mastering them not only makes a marked contribution to perfecting ones abilities in self-defence, it also moves you one step further down the road towards Karate-Do. It is also a fact that you will never completely master a Kata. You are always on the way to doing this.

A further aspect should not go unmentioned – the aesthetics. It is not only the work and effort that accompanies the training, it is also simply fun to practice the Kata or to watch a demonstration of Kata. To the observer, the Kata have the effect of a particular kind of fascination, more than perhaps in the other sides of Karate.

The aesthetics of an excellently performed Kata in training or in a competition cannot simply be ignored. If a Kata has been performed perfectly, it is quite noticeable how much energy is expressed in this form of fighting against several imaginary opponents. The tension, speed, precision, dynamics, power and explosiveness of the techniques – a good Kata demonstration brings the whole variation of Karate to the fore.

The special characteristics of a particular style are reflected in the Kata. In Shotokan Karate there is a large spectrum of different Kata. The focus of the Kata in our style lies mainly more on the dynamic, rapid and explosive movements. Nevertheless, the 26 Kata in Shotokan are divided into two categories: those, which tend to be more rapid and explosive in the Shorin tradition, and those, which concentrate on the breathing and power side of the Shorei tradition. The Shorin group includes the Heian Katas, Empi, Bassai-Dai, Kanku-Dai, Nijushiho and the Gojushiho Kata. They also concentrate on the breathing techniques and consist of rather slower sequences, but the basic tempo is rapid and dynamic. Those, which concentrate more on power are in the Shorei group e.g., Jion and Hangetsu as well as Sochin and Jitte.

This book contains the advanced Master Kata Sochin, Meikyo, Chinte, Kanku-Sho, Wankan, Ji'in, Gankaku and Unsu. The Kata Unsu, Kanku-Sho and Sochin belong to the most favourite of all the competition Kata.

In addition, this book includes a description of the most important of the stances and also details of some typical movements that are repetitive.

May I wish all readers, who want to come to terms more intensively with the fascinating Master Kata in Shotokan Karate, lots of fun in reading the lessons here and good luck with Karate-Do.

1   Introduction

1.1   The History of Shotokan Karate

The origins of Karate lie in Okinawa. Far away from the Japanese mainland is the island, whose inhabitants, centuries ago, developed fighting techniques, which they used to defend themselves from invaders and armed aggressors. Through healthy trade connections and with it cultural exchanges with other Asian neighbouring countries, a heterogeneous martial art emerged out of the already existing local weapon and fighting techniques. The economic centres of Shuri, Naha and Tomari were where this development was focussed.

Martial arts on Okinawa became increasingly popular in 1429, after the ban on weapons was decreed by the King Sho Shin. Before even the Chinese influence of Chuan-Fa had gained a foothold on the island, the martial art of Te (Te = hand) was being taught by several masters. This occurred, however, in small schools and closed circles. It cannot be assumed that this martial art was standardised or, from today's standpoint, that it was a fully developed art.

In 1372, in the vicinity of Naha, several Chinese families settled and they brought martial arts and the religion of Buddhism with them. It is said that they had an influence on Te throughout the area of Naha. It is held that the local popular Naha-Te (later called Shorei-Ryu – 'Ryu' means 'school') was inspired from the traditions of Chuan-Fa – Chinese boxing. It consists of dynamic movements and lays value on breathing and the technique for the production of rapid and explosive power. The interest in Chinese culture amongst the Okinawans was large, and as a result the philosophy and the fighting techniques of Chinese boxing (also called Kempo) spread into several regions of Okinawa. Other centres for Te were Tomari and Shuri (the styles developed here were later also called Shorin-Ryu). A Chinese influence could also be found in the techniques with emphasis on breathing control and round defensive movements. Tomari-Te contains both these elements.

Because the inhabitants of Okinawa lived mainly as farmers, fishermen or traders, the specific characteristics of the old style can be related to the different traditions of their professions. The farming community preferred a style with a low stance posture so that they could defend themselves with the arms and the legs from low positions. Another powerful style with numerous arm movements can be traced to fishing traditions.

The farmers and the fishermen were also inventive in using their work implements as weapons. *Kobudo*, the use of a Bo, the Tonfa, Nunchaku, Kama and other items as implements being adapted as weapons comes from this epoch. Today's Kata still contain, in part, (defensive) movements against such weapons.

The Japanese occupied Okinawa in 1609 and subjugated the inhabitants. This led to a ban on Te under the Satsuma dynasty at the time of Iesha SHIMAZU, which as a result could only be practised in secrecy. Nevertheless, there were several masters, who taught their art further directly to their students. The fighting techniques were intertwined as a sort of code into the Kata. Training was also done using the Makiwara, where techniques could be executed with full contact. The necessity, in daily life, to be able to put down an armed aggressor using a decisive technique – even to kill him – came out in the whole system of training. This concentrated and focussed on vital points of the body and this played an important role.

The masters of this art were well respected in the community, but they were not a bit the almighty. It is therefore futile to philosophically glorify the beginnings back in the dark ages of this martial art or to try to justify the origins historically. Missing written evidence make any statement in this way merely speculative. It is, however, a fact that the fighting system, created by the fishermen and farmers of Okinawa, served above all one purpose: to be able to kill an enemy, who was superior both in weaponry and equipment, in order to survive.

The reforms of the Meiji government, which superseded the Satsuma reign in 1872, permitted the development of martial arts and their popularity throughout the whole country. In those days, the basic martial art that we know as Karate was called *"Okinawa-Te"* or *"Tang-Te"*. The latter of these two descriptions (*"Tang"* means *Chinese*) expressed the high respect held for anything coming from China. Te, as it was then, is not yet held by most historians as a complete or even standardised martial art. Completely differing styles had been developed in the various areas. Some consisted of very few techniques, which had been practised for years and years. Some Masters of the art even possessed a very limited repertoire. Some sources report that they practised only one to three techniques for the whole of their lives, but these were carried out to perfection.

There were often rivalries between the different schools and conflicts often broke out between the followers, having a negative influence on the reputation of martial arts.

The image of martial art, however, began to change once Te became a sport in the school curriculum. The young Master Gichin FUNAKOSHI left behind a great impression on some civil servants, when he gave a demonstration of his skills, and Te was introduced as a school sport in Okinawa in 1902. Thus the corner stone was laid for a change in the martial art, which started out as a mere method of survival and was fast becoming a type of popular sport. The reason, at that time, for the inclusion of Karate in the school curriculum is interesting: Karate was counted as being conducive to training the concentration and physical condition of the pupils. The self-defence aspect was more in the background.

Gichin FUNAKOSHI, born 1868, very quickly reached a great popularity and moved to Japan, where he stayed for the rest of his life developing modern Karate with great success. He was a student of the Masters AZATO and ITOSU, and using his great knowledge he developed not only modern Karate but also the Shotokan style. He 'japanised' also the original term *"Tang"*, borrowed from the Chinese (*"Tang-Te"* means *"Chinese hand"*), and instigated the Japanese character and term turning it into *"Kara"* (*"Kara"* means *"empty"*). This happened also as a reaction to the increasing self-awareness of the Japanese and their dissociation from Chinese influences. The term "Kara", however, equally includes the philosophical principles – the way to perfection of the character and the unification of the body and the soul – that are integrated into this martial art.

In 1917, after FUNAKOSHI had demonstrated his style of martial art in Japan for the first time at the behest of the government, the impetus this gave to Karate knew no bounds. He pursued his aim – spreading the art of Karate – with inexhaustible zealousness and this made him even more successful. This was because he had become a highly well-informed Master, who was not only venerated because of his Karate expertise, but who also enjoyed popularity in high governmental circles and with the royal family. FUNAKOSHI also worked as a successful calligraphist and author, publishing his works under the nom de plume of "Shoto". He was well known in Japan and increasingly found new followers, above all many from universities as well as from military circles. His popularity in the universities helped his Karate teaching later to reach world-wide popularity, as many of his students at the universities were destined to go abroad later.

In addition to the long tradition of the predominant Kata form of Karate training, in the 1930s, FUNAKOSHI developed training with a partner, Gohon Kumite, Kihon Ippon Kumite, Jiyu Ippon Kumite and free fighting. He extracted sequences from the Kata and these were exercised with a partner using various techniques. In Kihon, additional techniques were practised, which were not contained in the Kata. In this way a programme was created that came very close to self-defence. Kata training was now devoted more to the aim of achieving flexibility, speed and strengthening of the muscles. Aesthetic dimensions were also gradually being taken into account. The daily routine practice of Karate in three elements that we know today of Kihon, Kumite and Kata, came about at that time.

In the 1930s, further styles of Karate, such as Goju-Ryu, Shito-Ryu and Wado-Ryu had been developed in addition to the style of Shotokan Karate. These styles were also introduced by Masters from Okinawa.

In honour of FUNAKOSHI, several influential friends built a Dojo, which they named "Shotokan". This means "The hall of Shoto" and was from then on the term used for his style. The symbol for Shotokan Karate, the tiger in a circle, was designed by the famous artist Hoan KOSUGI, a friend of FUNAKOSHI, to illustrate his books about Karate. This is also the symbol widely used and adopted globally by Shotokan Karate clubs and associations still today.

After the end of the war, in 1949, the *"Japan Karate Association"* (JKA) was founded and with it the joint organisation of all the Dojos, Karate Groups and University schools in the whole of Japan that practised FUNAKOSHI's Shotokan style. The "Japan Karate Association" (JKA) became the Association for all Shotokan Karateka in Japan and later world-wide. The other styles had also formed their own associations. The JKA Organisation's symbol − called *Inyo* − remains the small dark circle in the larger clear circle right up to today. It represents the duality of the universe, and embodies, similar to the symbolism of Yin and Yang, the opposing forces of the universe.

The fact that Shotokan spread world-wide so fast is mainly due to the development of instructor programmes at the Takushoku University. It was here in the 1950s, in a commercially and technically oriented university, that a stiff and demanding education programme was carried out, in which only the best Karate students could take part, who were destined afterwards to be employed internationally. The programme of instruction was drawn up, under the supervision of FUNAKOSHI, by

NAKAYAMA, OKAZAKI and NISHUAMA. These people were in leading positions in the JKA and were responsible for the sporting development of the Association. Together with FUNAKOSHI, they gave Karate demonstrations to American soldiers, amongst others, on the US Air Force bases. Later, the JKA sent 30 of their best instructors round the world, in order to spread the teaching of Shotokan Karate. Amongst them were well known Karate Masters such as KANAZAWA, KASE, SHIRAI, NISHIJAMA, OKAZAKI, MIKAMI, OKAMOTO, KAWAZOE, NAITO, OCHI and ENOEDA.

The development of the Shotokan style and the high technical standards of the JKA stayed under FUNAKOSHI's direction as the Karate repertoire, the scholastic foundation of the Karate techniques and the introduction of competitive Karate were brought to their heights. Masatoshi NAKAYAMA inherited all this after FUNAKOSHI's death in 1957 and he was named as the highest official in the JKA. After his studies he had lived a long time in China and brought new techniques from there.

He also studied the lesser-known styles and integrated the essentials into the Shotokan system, e.g., the original Goju-Ryu Kata Hangetsu. In the 1930's NAKAYAMA had already received the task to learn the Gojushiho Kata and Nijushiho of the Master MABUNI and adapt them for the Shotokan style. Together with FUNAKOSHI and his son Giko, who had introduced the Sochin Kata, NAKAYAMA continued with the development of the system to create a complete martial art, and this soon included all the important elements. In Shotokan, there are not only the simple and rapid elements of the Shorin-Ryu present, but also the powerful and emphasised breathing system of the Shorei-Ryu as well.

The instructor's text books, which have been written, in particular NAKAYAMA's works, laid the foundation later to spread the techniques in the style to a broad public.

At the same time, the competition, just like in other Budo disciplines, was brought in as an effective means of advertising the sport. By the 1950s, all the main Karate styles had generated free fighting and had now begun to produce rule systems like those that already existed in Judo, Kendo and other martial arts sports. The concept of carrying out competitions in Budo sports is not specific to Karate alone and the idea was also not conceived by the JKA. Judo, Kendo and other Budo arts were further advanced in this respect than Karate at that time. These martial arts had also successfully managed to integrate a sporting component into their system. In 20th century Japan, it was no longer necessary to have to kill someone using the martial arts in order to survive, unlike life in the pre-Meiji regime 19th century period. In addition, the sportsman should be protected against injury by a meaningful set of rules, without which they already had suffered for a long time with comparative injuries anyway.

After a five-year test phase, in 1956, the JKA came out with its first rule book and in 1957 the first All-Japan Masters Championship was carried out. The difficulties in defining the competition rules that the organising instructors, NISHIJAMA, NAKAYAMA and others, ran up against was to ban from the match the numerous dangerous techniques. These were, in any case often hardly, if not at all, controllable, but the secret was to stay as far as possible within the traditions of Karate-Do. In addition to Kumite competitions, the JKA instructors also created rules for the Kata discipline.

The concept of competition being included in the repertoire of JKA Shotokan Karate stayed under the leadership of FUNAKOSHI, who was at the head of the JKA until his death in 1957. The father of modern Karate knew that this aspect was also important in order to anchor the longevity of Karate as a Martial Art in Japan alongside the other Budo disciplines. However, despite this he was also critical about these developments. FUNAKOSHI was not particularly conservative in his handling of Karate. He was only interested in spreading his style. To do this he had already brought in many innovations, reforms and breaks with the Okinawan tradition in order to perfect his system.

He had already adapted Karate in 1902 from the original idea of the *"art of killing in order to survive"* to being a school sport. He had changed the names of the Kata and 'Japanised' the term *"Karate"* and the names of the Kata – all much against the insistence of the Okinawan Masters. In order to create a unified martial arts system and to bring it to be accepted in Japan, the competition had to be one aspect amongst many. This is why the match bout represents the last brick in building the development of the Shotokan system.

FUNAKOSHI stayed, nevertheless, sceptical regarding an interpretation of Karate that was only based on a question of success in sport. In an interview about FUNAKOSHI's standpoint about the introduction of competition, NAKAYAMA said: "He was very concerned that, if competition became too popular, then students would ignore the basic principles and only train for the match bout. He realised that there would be competitions and that they would be important in making Karate internationally popular. However, he also wanted to make it clear that the basic schooling and training must be the prime important point."

Since the JKA and those Karate Associations, who followed the JKA tradition, wanted to dispel these fears of FUNAKOSHI, they maintain a priority for Kata and Kihon and see the competition as merely a facet of Karate-Do.

The reason for the development of a sporting dimension in Karate is not due to a "westernisation" of Karate. The arrival of the sporting bout reflected the social situation in Japan. Further reasons lay in the necessity to have it compared to other sports governed by rules, as well considerations on the effectiveness of publicising the sport.

Although Karate today is not thinkable without the *"Shiai"* – the competition – only a very small minority practise Karate also as a competitive sport. Subsequently, this aspect of Karate is only, in effect, a widening of the horizon belonging to those practising Karate. Whether it be Kata or Kumite, sporting success would not be possible in a Karate competition without a high degree of self-discipline and concentration. This is what lies behind the thought of "Ikken Hissatsu" – killing with a single blow – in the philosophy of the Ippon in competitions. In addition there is the discipline and respect for the opponent. All this in maintaining the tradition of Karate-Do.

Taking part in competitions is the whetstone on which the razor sharpness in Karate is honed. With realistic situations and fair rules and conditions, this makes it possible for the Karateka to study the effectiveness of his techniques or his mental preparation. Almost all of the great Japanese and western Karate Masters have a successful period as competitors behind them. The time spent on competitions, however, should lead from the finish of such a phase for the Karateka through to Karate-Do as an accompanying life-style.

In the year of the first Japanese Masters Championships – 1957 – FUNAKOSHI died at the age of almost 90. According to reports by JKA Instructor Teruyuki OKAZAKI, he was still giving instruction in the Central Dojo of the JKA every day right up to a few days before his death. The JKA continued with FUNAKOSHI's aim – the spreading of Shotokan Karate – with world-wide success under the leadership of Masatoshi NAKAYAMA.

NAKAYAMA has laid down in his books the mandatory standards for the techniques, sequences and application of the Shotokan Kata, which are still maintained today. These were defined at a meeting held in 1948 for universities in Japan practising Shotokan. The Kata illustrated in this book draw largely on his interpretation.

The interpretation of Karate by the JKA, quite rightly, is still today the model example for the majority of the estimated several million Karateka, world-wide, following the Shotokan style. The high standard of the JKA technical guidelines – including the Kata interpretations – are still today the ones, which remain accepted world-wide for the Shotokan style.

Today it is generally recognised that the attraction of traditional Karate-Do lies in the fact that it fulfils a variety of demands; Karate is a broad-spectrum sport for all age groups; or as a Martial Art for self-defence; or as a way to the inner-self or as a competitive sport. The reasons for carrying out the Martial Art Karate-Do are as varied as the mentality and make-up of the human, who practises it. Above all, however, it is the respect and courtesy for others, which should be paramount. The question of which is the 'correct' main area of Karate cannot be definitively answered.

All facets of Karate-Do today can be interesting and valuable for the development and self-esteem of the individual. Which main area one will specialise on is up to the person himself and the phase reached in progressing along the path of life. Karate means different things to different people. It is, nevertheless, important to find one's own way and to tolerate other Karate lines, since Karate-Do offers an enormous variety of possibilities.

1.2   Karate-Do

Brought about by the changes in Okinawa-Te into a Japanese martial art, it combined itself more and more with the ethical and spiritual influence of Japan. This martial art stems from an era, when it was still used as a 'weapon' for the Okinawan farmers and fishermen. In those days the origins had nothing to do with anything philosophical or even related to the Samurai. The techniques used by the inhabitants of Okinawan revealed no spiritual or ethical influence. The problem for the farmer and the fisherman was one of survival. Only later, when the simple question of survival was no longer a requirement, and when the Japanese, as well as the other Martial Arts, began to influence things, did Karate begin to integrate the strong philosophical elements.

This gave the term *"Do"* a special meaning. In English, the word *"Do"* means *"way"*. Just like in Karate, other Martial Arts such as Judo, Kendo and Aikido, amongst many, use the same term in conjunction with the main name of the art. In the 19th Century, these Budo Arts still had the word *"Jutsu"* (meaning 'technique') added.

Respectively Kenjutsu and Karate-Jutsu were the "techniques with the sword" or the "techniques with the empty hand". The compulsion to use techniques, which are traced back to the idea of killing in self-defence, lies behind this terminology. The late 19th Century Japan saw this necessity no longer existing. In numerous Kenjutsu schools, at that time, competitions using the bamboo sword *"Shinai"* took place and these quickly became popular, leading to the name *"Kendo"* being used. The changeover from the original term *"sword technique"* to *"way of the sword"* was determined by the new social circumstances, in which these arts handed down from the Samurai were now practised.

"Do" describes the way to mastering the art. This is the long 'road', which should bring about the improvement of the character and the technical skills by not only having the aim of mastering the discipline, but, moreover, by working on the psychical and physical attributes of the sportsman's personality. Continuous work on oneself is the way and not the vision of the end product.

This would mean that the aim of training would not be towards the highest degree of performance in the sport, but would be the *"way"* – exercising that is. FUNAKOSHI coined this by saying; "The main aim in the art of Karate is neither winning nor losing – it is the improvement of the character". This expresses the lifelong striving to perfect the control of the body and mind. Karate techniques and the grade reached in mastering them are merely a reflection of the inner-self at that particular time. *"Mushin"* – an open mind without having to think – is a mental process, which should help the pupil to progress down this difficult path.

FUNAKOSHI drew attention to the entity of the philosophy of Do in Karate using the 20 paragraphs. They serve to help the student in his search for perfection and in developing his individual potential. Although practice and training is the nucleus of Do, the execution of a practice exercise does not necessarily serve to learn the skill. It serves above all to enrich life through awareness and knowledge.

In his book "Shotokan no Hyakkajiten", SCHLATT (1995) lists FUNAKOSHI's 20 principles, which define the entity of Karate-Do as a model:

*   Never forget: Karate starts with the Rei and ends with the Rei.
    (Rei means veneration and respect).
*   In Karate there is no pre-emptive strike.
    (In Karate you don't attack first).
*   Karate aids on the road to fairness.

INTRODUCTION

- First of all know yourself and then the others.
- Body and spirit come before technique.
- Learn to control your body and mind and keep it clear.
- Negligence causes harm.
- Karate doesn't take place only in the Dojo.
- Learning Karate is a life-long task.
- Combine your daily routine with Karate – that is the secret.
- True Karate is like hot water, which cools rapidly if you don't keep it constantly warm.
- Don't think about winning all the time, but think about how not to lose.
- Gauge yourself according to your opponent.
- The fight is dependent on the exploitation of successes and misses.
- Imagine your hand and your feet are swords.
- When you exit the gateway of youth, you'll find you have many opponents.
- Moving to adopt a stance is what a beginner does, later it becomes a natural act.
- Practice the Kata correctly, in a real fight it will be another thing.
- Hard and soft, tension and relaxation, slow and fast – everything with the correct breathing.
- Always think about what you are doing and constantly try something new.

Politeness, respect and the defensive characteristics of Karate, which are anchored as the main theme in FUNAKOSHI's principles, are all symbolised in the emblem of Shotokan Karate. The tiger in the circle illustrates the principles of Karate-Do. The tiger represents the ability to fight and to win, but it's freedom and aggressiveness is limited by the confines of the circle. The circle represents patience, consideration, reasonability, understanding and control – all the essence of Karate-Do. These characteristics should be your constant companion in your routine, daily training.

1.3   Kata

The Kata typify the variety found in Karate. Techniques, which can be used at all the fighting distances to the opponent, can be found in them. This is why your training sessions take on a large importance.

The Kata – as already said – concisely express the self-defence techniques of the time, when Okinawa-Te was still forbidden in the form of combat against several imaginary opponents. *"Form"*, or the more freely interpreted expression *"Sequences"*, is the correct translation for the term *"Kata"*. After 1900, as Karate was quickly spreading in interest, the contemporary styles we know today came into existence and shaped each of the various systems according to each individual understanding of the art of Kata. There are estimated to be up to 80 Kata in existence in all.

Shotokan teaches 26 Kata, not counting the preliminary exercise forms. Originally Gichin FUNAKOSHI selected 15 Kata, which he held as central to the training for Shotokan. They contained the individual typical traditions of the Shorin and Shorei schools. Belonging to these Kata were the basic Kata Heian Shodan, Heian Nidan, Heian Sandan, Heian Yondan and Heian Godan. One assumes that they were developed from the complex Kata Kanku-Dai in order to afford beginners a systematic and simplified introduction to the sequences and techniques. These basic Kata stem from the Shorin school, whose Masters taught the principle of rapid and powerful movements. Originally they were called *"Pinan"* Kata until Funakoshi renamed them *"Heian"*, which means *"peace"* and *"calm"*. For him, the three Tekki-Kata also belonged to the central Kata such as Bassai-Dai, Kanku-Dai, Empi, Gankaku, Jitte, Hangetsu and Jion. Several further Kata came later on such as Gojushiho-Kata and Sochin. Today there are 26 Kata in Shotokan Karate:

Basic Kata:
Heian 1-5, Tekki 1-3.

Master Kata:
Bassai-Dai, Jion, Empi, Hangetsu, Kanku-Dai.

Advanced Master Kata:
Jitte, Meikyu, Ji'in, Bassai-Sho, Kanku-Sho, Gankaku, Chinte, Wankan, Nijushiho, Gojushiho-Sho, Gojushiho-Dai, Sochin, Unsu.

Each Kata illustrates a laid down, defined and complete element and consists of a typical fighting repertoire with a typical rhythm and a typical degree of difficulty. As a general rule, the Kata increase, as one moves up the scale, in complexity and the number of techniques and steps. Thus the first Kata – Heian Shodan – consists of 21 movements, Heian Nidan has 26 movements and Heian Yondan 27. Common in all the Kata is the fighting shout 'Kiai', which is uttered at specifically laid down points. This is the way that the whole Kime of the techniques unfolds. The 'Kiai' is uttered at those places in the Kata where a decisive counter-attack comes. In the Kata this means a dramatic highpoint, by which time certain movements must have been successfully executed i.e., a "Chapter" in the Kata or the whole Kata is completed.

A further common point in the Kata is the presence of a laid down sequence of steps (Enbusen). This means that direction and sequence have to be always the same. The starting stance must also match the end of the Kata. The Kata always begin with the formal greeting in Musubi-Dachi – this is the stance where the heels are together. After this the prepared position Hachi-Dachi is adopted. Each change of direction is accompanied and preceded by a change of the direction of the eyes.

Present at all times in the Kata, however, is the principle that "Karate ni sente nashi" is maintained – this means "There is no first strike in Karate". As a result all Kata begin with a defensive technique. This doesn't exclude that in some Kata, a direct counter can be interpreted as being used as the opponent starts to attack.

In the training for the Kata, it is important that, first of all, a good standard of Kihon is reached before one starts with the actual Kata training. At the beginning, the sequence of the Kata is practised slowly. Correct turns, techniques and stances are now critical, while powerful and dynamic execution comes later. After the sequence has been mastered, then these components come into play. Let's add to that: This is when it gets really interesting! Dynamics, rhythm and expression in the Kata performance can only be carried out on the basis of a flawless internalisation of the sequence. The appreciation of the meaning of the technique being carried out adds yet another dimension.

The fascinating thing about Kata training is the constant increase of new experiences that one can still find in doing the exercises. One can never master a Kata completely. It's more like you will get somewhere near perfecting it. It goes without saying that "perfect" must be seen as a relative statement. Different people carrying out the same Kata will execute it in different ways. It's not about the sequence of the technique or the rhythm, which are of course laid down. Size, weight, stature, body type, age, sex, elasticity and other factors all have an influence on the differences. Every good trainer or competition referee will take account of these in his assessment; he will recognise the individual qualities and grade the Kata performance accordingly i.e., whether the Karateka has achieved the highest possible advantage from his individual attempt.

The Kata performance must be correct and bring out the dynamic, fighting spirit and explosiveness in the right place. The rapid and slow movements as well as tension and relaxation must also be accounted for. Breathing-in and breathing-out at the correct moments are similarly elementary criteria for the assessment. If a Kata is carried out too quickly, it's speciality goes often lost. High grade Kata experts demonstrate their Kata properly. They can tell a story with their Kata performance and this will bring out the essence of them.

How intensive the applications are brought into training is a question that has many varied answers. The opinion of many Karate trainers is that generally Karateka, who are taking their training seriously, will almost always decide for themselves which applications they will use. This is certainly the case for many of the simple blocking and attack techniques. The feeling for other, more complex techniques is not quite so clearly apparent. One has to practice with a partner to understand the potentiality of which application is best to use.

A further aspect is that many techniques are of a pure symbolic nature, while others must be practised very slowly and with great care in order not to injure the partner. When training for the Bunkai, there are as many different opinions as there are possibilities for using the applications in each of the techniques. Here it is well understood that whichever is not necessarily the only version possible.

Thus, just as there are a number of applications for the first movement in the first Kata, it is also important to register that there is no perfect solution, rather each will have it's own justification. The same applies to the variety of training methods. It is also quite in order to see the purpose of Kata training more as being the schooling generally of flexibility, co-ordination, rhythm, the aesthetics of the movement and finally condition. The self-defence aspects can be covered by the classic Karate-Kumite, while, on the other side of the coin, it's possible that the Bunkai can be concentrated on more.

Training tips for learning the Kata:

- Requirement: All the stances and techniques contained in the Kata have already been mastered.
- First of all, practice the sequence slowly, and watch out for the correct movement of the hips.
- Practise the change of position (turn) and direction of the eyes.
- Timing, power, dynamics, fighting spirit are introduced only after the sequence has been mastered.
- After that, the understanding for the application can be increased by training with a partner.
- In order to improve the Kata, training in front of a mirror, like those available in many Dojos, can be of great assistance.
- Individual elements of the Kata should be repeated and practised as long as it takes to master them.
- Those Kata that you have already learned should be repeated, slowly, but with full effort, in order to maintain your repertoire.
- Don't carry out a Kata in a hasty fashion. Kata tell a story. Any good story has an introduction, a climax and a conclusion.
- Don't begin a new Kata too soon. The ability to master a Kata takes several months, if not years, and cannot be learned in a short time.
- Whenever the opportunity exists, take part in a Kata tournament. They constitute an excellent exercise to test yourself under stress conditions and to see whether you are able to execute it without a mistake.

The higher the grading is, the more a comprehensive repertoire of Kata must be mastered. In my opinion, training for the sequences and an understanding of timing, co-ordination and the fine points all come as a priority in Kata training. Moreover, the meaning of each technique must be understood. How far one gets to grips on how the techniques are used in practice is dependent on the time that one can devote to Karate.

Independent from this, whichever main theme one chooses for Kata training and how intensive one wants to get involved in the Bunkai, there is nothing mysterious or secret in the Kata techniques and their practice in the Bunkai form. They are used in mainly simple and practical self-defence situations.

The understanding for the Kata takes a lot of time and not everyone can spend so much time on intensively carrying out Karate-Do that would otherwise perhaps be necessary to completely master it. Therefore you simply have to exercise much patience and don't despair, when, after several years, you still cannot cover equally all the ground in Karate. Karate-Do is a long-term project and not something that one can master in two or three years.

Mastering the fascinating 26 Shotokan Kata is a challenge, which can be taken up with new experiences every time. Kata make it possible to have a lifelong practice companion, unlike other disciplines, in which the zenith of performance is reached at a particular age – the conscious practice of the Kata will always see a steady improvement.

Notes to the Kata descriptions:

Each Kata begins and ends with a bow – the Rei. The heels are close together during this movement. Then one adopts the natural Shizentai position at the Hachi-Dachi. At the same time as the right leg comes into this position, the arms are crossed over in a short defensive movement. In the Yoi position the arms are held directly in front of the thighs.

The techniques Oi-Zuki and Gyaku-Zuki are generally carried out at the Chudan region height in the Kata. If a different height is required (Gedan or Jodan), then this is indicated additionally in the texts.

Side or Front views are shown in the Kata sequences in the oval illustrations in order to create clarity.

2 The Master Kata

2.1   Meikyo

Apart from one exception, this Kata calls for no technique that possesses any particularly demanding movement. Meikyo is a Kata, which uses measures to ward off attacks by sticks in its main section. In this respect it is similar to the Kata Bassai-Sho and Jitte, which also contain the principles of defending, grasping and wresting against attacks by the long stick (Bo). The outstanding characteristic of this Kata is the jump movement Sankaku Tobi. In this, one avoids the opponent's attack by using a turning jump and by countering during the dodging movement. Earlier, Meikyo was also called Rohai. In the version taught by NAKAYAMA, which can be seen in this book, it is executed using only Gedan-Barai and Uchi-Uke. Meikyo was one of NAKAYAMA's favourite Kata. In the version taught by KANAZAWA it uses Gedan-Barai, Uchi-Uke and Age-Uke.

Sequence of actions:

(1) Shizentai.

(2) Bring the feet together with the right coming alongside the left, while at the same time lifting the arms upwards. The hands are open.

(3) Keeping the same stance drop down into a Kiba-Dachi position while crossing the arms over the head and bringing the hands down onto the hips.

(4) Remaining in the same position slowly bring the hands together in front of the face, and

(5) then, execute a Kakiwake-Uke block to the outside.

(6) Turn left 45° into a Zenkutsu-Dachi position and do a left Gedan-Barai.

(7) Go forward right into a Zenkutsu-Dachi position doing an Oi-Zuki.

(8) Pull the right foot back a little, and then turn right 90° into a right-footed Zenkutsu-Dachi position doing a Gedan-Barai.

(9) Go forward left into a Zenkutsu-Dachi position doing an Oi-Zuki.

(10) Bring the right foot forward a little, preparing for a Bo-Uke and then,

(11) go forward 45° into a right-footed Kokutsu-Dachi position with a Bo-Uke.

(12) Take a gliding step forward into a right Zenkutsu-Dachi position with a Bo-Tsukami (grab the stick and push).

(13) Turn round rearwards on the spot into a left Zenkutsu-Dachi position, at the same time "wresting the stick from your opponent". Your eyes are still looking in the same direction as before.

(14) Look in the opposite direction, pulling the right foot slowly forward and at the same time lift both arms upwards again.

(15) Move the right foot slowly sideways into a Kiba-Dachi position and at the same time cross the arms above the head and bring them down on to the hips.

(16) Turn left 45° into a left Zenkutsu-Dachi position doing a Gedan-Barai.

(17) Go forward right into a Zenkutsu-Dachi position doing an Oi-Zuki.

(18) Bring the right foot back a little, and then go 90° into a right-footed Zenkutsu-Dachi position doing a Gedan-Barai.

(19) Go forward into a left-footed Zenkutsu-Dachi position doing an Oi-Zuki.

(20) Bring the right foot forward a little, preparing for a Bo-Uke and then,

(21) go forward 45° into a right Kokutsu-Dachi position with a Bo-Uke.

(22) Take a gliding step forward into a right Zenkutsu-Dachi position with a Bo-Tsukami (grab the stick and push).

(23) Turn round rearwards on the spot into a left Zenkutsu-Dachi position, at the same time "wresting the stick from your opponent". Your eyes are still looking in the same direction as before.

(24) Look in the opposite direction, pulling the right foot slowly forward and at the same time lift both arms upwards again.

(25) Move the right foot slowly sideways into a Kiba-Dachi position and at the same time cross the arms above the head and bring them down on to the hips.

(26) Turn left 45º into a left Zenkutsu-Dachi position doing an Uchi-Uke.

(27) Go forward right into a Zenkutsu-Dachi position doing an Oi-Zuki.

(28) Bring the right foot back a little, and then go 90º to the right into a right-footed Zenkutsu-Dachi position doing an Uchi-Uke.

(29) Go forward into a left-footed Zenkutsu-Dachi position doing an Oi-Zuki.

(30) Eyes are looking forward over the left shoulder and bring the left foot forward, preparing for a Tettsui-Uchi.

(31) Turn left 45º into a Kiba-Dachi position doing a Tettsui-Uchi.

(32) Do a right Mikazuki-Geri onto the open left hand. **KIAI.**

(33) Place the right leg backwards into a left-footed Kokutsu-Dachi position at the same time ripping the arms down to the sides.

(34) Remaining in the same position place both fists on top of each other on the right hip.

(35) Morote-Haiwan-Uke.

(36) Step forward and pull back ready for a Morote-Haiwan-Uke.

(37) Go forward right into a Kokutsu-Dachi position with a Morote-Haiwan-Uke.

(38) Slowly step forward and cross both arms above the head.

(39) Go forward again slowly into a left Zenkutsu-Dachi position with a double side block.

(40) Step forward, pulling back for a double Uchi-Uke.

(41) In a right Kokutsu-Dachi position do a double Uchi-Uke.

(42) Take a gliding step forward at the same time punch out straight forward with both fists.

(43) Bring the arms back into a starting position.

(44) Turn round 180º on the spot to the rear and at the same time prepare for a left Age-Uke.

(45) Left Kokutsu-Dachi position with an Age-Uke.

(46) Jump round 180º well to the rear at the same time slap the right forearm against the flat of the left hand. **KIAI.**

(47) Land down in a right Kokutsu-Dachi position doing a Shuto-Uke.

(48) Step backwards into a left Kokutsu-Dachi with a Shuto-Uke.

(49) Shizentai.

Application for (2)-(5)

Application for (20)-(23)

Application for (45)-(47)

2.2 Sochin

Characteristic of this very aesthetic and powerful Kata is the prevalence of the Fudo-Dachi position also called the Sochin-Dachi position. This very firm and stable stance resembles the basic position also in Kumite with the rear leg bent. The switch over between fast and slow movements from the Fudo-Dachi position gives this Kata a very powerful character. Sochin is a very popular Kata and is often seen in competitions. Because the prevalent stance in the Kata is actually called the Fudo-Dachi, it would be quite wrong to think that the Kata derives its name from the stance. It is more likely that the stance derives its alternative name from the word Sochin. Translated, the two syllables of Sochin mean *robust, powerful* (So) and *suppress, hold down, calm down* (Chin). The history of the Kata assumes that FUNAKOSHI's son had integrated this Kata into the Shotokan system.

Sequence of actions:

(1) Shizentai.

(2) Slowly go forward to the right and at the same time pull back for a double-block Jodan-Uke and Gedan-Uke.

(3) Remaining in the same position sink your body down in two movements.

(4) Go forward right into a Fudo-Dachi position with a left Jodan-Uke and a right Gedan-Uke. In the Gedan-Uke the arm is slightly bent.

(5) Switch your weight forwards and pull slowly back with the right arm for a Tate-Shuto-Uke.

(6) Go forward slowly into a left-footed Fudo-Dachi with a right Tate Shuto-Uke. As you do this try to twist the hips round without moving the position of your legs.

(7) Remaining in the same position do an Oi-Zuki.

(8) Remaining in the same position do a Gyaku-Zuki.

(9) Look 90º to the left and pull back for a Manji-Uke.

(10) Left forward into a Kokutsu-Dachi position with a Manji-Uke.

(11) Go forward into a right-footed Fudo-Dachi with a double-block, left with a Jodan-Uke and right with a Gedan-Uke. In the Gedan-Uke the arm is slightly bent.

(12) Go forward slowly into a left-footed Fudo-Dachi with a right Tate Shuto-Uke.

(13) Remaining in the same position do an Oi-Zuki.

(14) Remaining in the same position do a Gyaku-Zuki.

(15) Place the left leg to the rear and look backwards over the left shoulder, pulling back for a Manji-Uke.

(16) Turn round 180º in to a left-footed Kokutsu-Dachi position doing a Manji-Uke.

(17) Go forward into a right-footed Fudo-Dachi with a double-block, left with a Jodan-Uke and right with a Gedan-Uke. In the Gedan-Uke the arm is slightly bent.

(18) Go forward slowly into a left-footed Fudo-Dachi with a right Tate Shuto-Uke.

(19) Remaining in the same position do an Oi-Zuki.

(20) Remaining in the same position do a Gyaku-Zuki.

(21) Pull the left leg backwards. Turn round rearwards 180º on the right leg and snap the left knee upwards. Lay the fists, one over the other, onto the right hip.

(22) Do a Yoko-Geri-Keage whip-kick with the left leg together with a Uraken punch.

(23) Land into a left-footed Fudo-Dachi position with a right Mai-Empi into the open left hand.

(24) Look to the rear and lift the right knee up high while at the same time lay the fists, one over the other, onto the left hip.

(25) Do a Yoko-Geri-Keage whip-kick with the right leg together with a Uraken punch.

(26) Land into a right-footed Fudo-Dachi position with a left Mai-Empi into the open right hand.

(27) Look to the rear over the right shoulder and pull back for a right Shuto-Uke.

(28) Turn round to the rear 180º on the left leg into a right-footed Kokutsu-Dachi position doing a Shuto-Uke.

(29) Move forward 45º into a left-footed Kokutsu-Dachi position with a Shuto-Uke.

(30) Turn round 135º to the left into a left footed Kokutsu-Dachi position with a Shuto-Uke.

(31) Move forward 45º into a right-footed Kokutsu-Dachi position with a Shuto-Uke.

(32) Change round 45º to the right into a right-footed Kokutsu-Dachi position with a Shuto-Uke.

(33) Move forward into a left-footed Kokutsu-Dachi position with a Shuto-Uke.

(34) Take a gliding step forward with a stabbing right Gyaku-Nukite and a left Osae-Uke block. In the Nukite position the palm of the hand is upwards. The stance adopted is a little higher than in the Kokutsu-Dachi position.

(35) Front view.

(36) Execute a Mae-Geri kick with the forward leg. The position of the arms is unchanged.

(37) Front view.

(38) Place the kicking leg back down and then immediately do a right-footed Mae-Geri. As the kick is executed pull the right forearm sharply back and the left arm moves forwards to prepare for a right Uraken-Uchi block and a left Nagashi-Uke block.

(39) Front view.

(40) Place the feet down in a right-footed Fudo-Dachi position with a right Uraken-Uchi block and a left Nagashi-Uke block. **KIAI.**

(41) Front view.

(42) Turn round rearwards 180º on the left leg and pull the right leg sharply up. Execute a Mikazuki-Geri into the left hand and prepare for a double block left with a Jodan-Uke and right with a Gedan-Uke.

(43) Land into a right-footed Fudo-Dachi position with a Fumikomi with a right Gedan-Uke and a left Jodan-Uke.

(44) Move forward left 45º into a left-footed Fudo-Dachi position with an Uchi-Uke.

(45) Move forward 45º into a right-footed Fudo-Dachi position with an Oi-Zuki.

(46) Bring the front leg forward to the other a little and twist round 90º to the right into a right-footed Fudo-Dachi position with an Uchi-Uke.

(47) Move forward into a left-footed Fudo-Dachi position with an Oi-Zuki.

(48) Move the front leg 45º to the left into a left-footed Fudo-Dachi position with an Uchi-Uke.

(49) Remaining in the same position do a Gyaku Uchi-Uke.

(50) Do a right Mae-Geri.

(51) Snap the leg back quickly and place it down to the rear in a left-footed Fudo-Dachi position. At the same time slowly punch the left fist forward for a Yumi-Zuki, and as you do this bring the right fist back onto the chest.

(52) Remaining in the same position do a Gyaku-Zuki.

(53) Remaining in the same position do an Oi-Zuki. **KIAI.**

(54) Shizentai.

Application for (4)

Application for (33)-(41)

Application for (42)-(43)

2.3   Jitte

The name Jitte means *ten hands* or, in the metaphorical sense *ten opponents*. This is aimed at expressing the ability to defend oneself against ten attackers if one knows this Kata. Jitte is possible without employing any kicking-techniques at all, if one excludes the stamping step for the Fumikomi.

Just like Jion and Ji'in, having some of the same basic techniques in common, Jitte is in the category of the more powerful Kata. Whether Jitte, Jion and Ji'in are variants of one and the same Kata, as is assumed now and then, is not clear. The prevalent techniques against the attacker armed with the Bo show similarities with Bassai-Sho and Meikyo. Jitte is a very short Kata, which contains a variety of extraordinary techniques using the open hand. It is also taught, with specific interpretations of the techniques, in other styles.

Sequence of actions:

(1) Shizentai.

(2) Slowly bring the legs together and lay the right-hand fist into the open left hand.

(3) Open the hands and bring the left leg slowly backwards and prepare for a Tekubi-Osae-Uke.

(4) Right-footed Zenkutsu-Dachi with a Tekubi-Osae-Uke. The hands are held as in the Teisho block.

(5) Look left 45º and slowly bring the left foot in a little and get ready to do a double Teisho-Uke.

(6) Carry on going forward slowly into a left-footed Zenkutsu-Dachi position doing a double Teisho-Uke.

(7) Look rearwards over the right shoulder and do a left-armed block support on to the right arm.

(8) Take a gliding step to the right into a Kiba-Dachi with a right Haito-Uchi.

(9) Look forward through 90º pulling in the right leg and prepare to do a right Teisho-Uchi.

(10) Go forward in a right Kiba-Dachi with a right-handed Teisho-Uchi.

(11) Step forward in a Kiba-Dachi position with a left-handed Teisho-Uchi.

(12) Take another step forward in a Kiba-Dachi position with a right-handed Teisho-Uchi.

(13) Look forward through 90° bringing the right leg in front of the left one and cross the arms over the head. Stay standing at the same height as before in the Kiba-Dachi.

(14) Go sideways to the left into a Kiba-Dachi position bringing both arms down to the sides.

(15) Bring the right foot into the left one and at the same time get ready for a double Jodan-Uchi-Uke.

(16) Left into a Kiba-Dachi position with a double Jodan-Uchi-Uke.

(17) Look rearwards over the right shoulder and turn on the right leg through 180º rearwards lifting the left leg up sharply for a Fumikomi. The arms remain as far as possible unchanged and the hips are as far back as possible.

(18) Place the foot down in a left Fumikomi in a Kiba-Dachi position with a double Jodan Uchi-Uke.

(19) Lift the right knee up rapidly and -

(20) - place it down forward and right with a Fumikomi in a Kiba-Dachi position with a double Jodan Uchi-Uke.

(21) Lift the left knee up rapidly and -

(22) - place it down forward and left with a Fumikomi in a Kiba-Dachi position with a double Jodan Uchi-Uke. **KIAI.**

(23) Look right, slowly bringing the right foot in a little and cross the arms over the head.

(24) Slowly stand upright and bring both arms down to the sides of the body.

(25) Go forward right getting ready to do a Jodan-Shuto-Uke.

(26) Go into a right-footed Zenkutsu-Dachi position with a Jodan-Shuto-Uke.

(27) Remaining in the same position execute a Bo-Uke (blocking a stick).

(28) Pull the left knee up slowly and at the same time lift the right hand up above the right shoulder and hold the left hand across the body to the right side.

(29) Front view.

(30) Place the left foot down into a Zenkutsu-Dachi position executing a Bo-Uke.

(31) Front view.

(32) Pull the right knee up slowly and at the same time lift the left hand up above the left shoulder and hold the right hand across the body to the left side.

(33) Place the right foot down into a Zenkutsu-Dachi position executing a Bo-Uke.

(34) Look over the left shoulder and turn through 270º on the right leg. At the same time get ready to do a Manji-Uke.

(35) Go forward left into a Kokutsu-Dachi position with a Manji-Uke.

(36) On the spot turn round directly in the opposite direction into a right-footed Kokutsu-Dachi position with a Manji-Uke.

(37) Look 90º forwards pulling in the left foot a little and get ready to do an Age-Uke.

(38) Go forward into a left-footed Zenkutsu-Dachi position with an Age-Uke.

(39) Go forward into a right-footed Zenkutsu-Dachi position with an Age-Uke.

(40) On the spot turn round 180º to the rear and get ready for a left Age-Uke.

(41) Do a left Age-Uke in a Zenkutsu-Dachi position.

(42) Go forward into a right-footed Zenkutsu-Dachi position with an Age-Uke. **KIAI.**

(43) Turn round rearwards slowly on the right leg and at the same time pull the left leg into the right one. The fist of the right hand lies in the left hand.

(44) Shizentai.

Application for (3)-(6)

Application for (7)-(8)

Application for (25)-(31)

2.4 Kanku-Sho

Kanku-Sho – the shorter *Kanku-Kata* – is quite naturally related to Kanku-Dai, but contains fewer techniques and as a result has a shorter sequence. Kanku-Sho is one of the most athletic Katas in the Shotokan system and it is a popular Kata for competitions. It poses a high challenge technically and requires fitness and athleticism from the Karateka. The two jumps contained in it are not the only characteristics in this Kata; the defensive techniques and the counter-attacks to the middle of the opponent's body are others. It is said that Master ITOSU, who developed this Kata, was fond of Chudan techniques and double-blocking techniques. This can be seen very clearly in this Kata. It is a typical Kata for Shotokan and is not taught in the other styles.

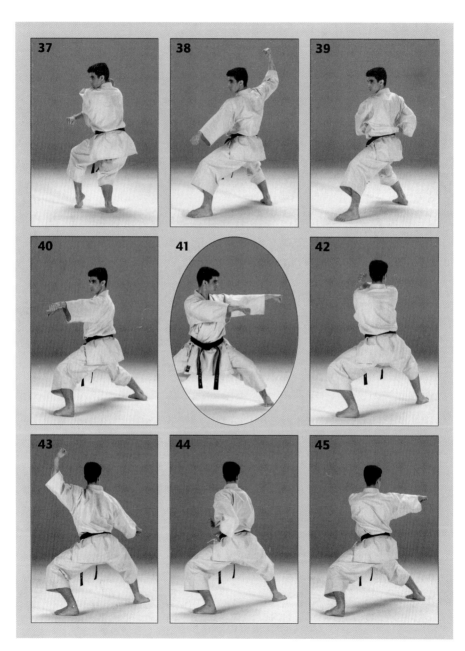

Sequence of actions:

(1) Shizentai.

(2) Look left and staying in the same position sink down a little preparing for a Morote-Uke.

(3) Take a sliding step to the right into a left-footed Kokutsu-Dachi position executing a Morote-Uke.

(4) Change the direction of the eyes to the right and prepare for a Morote-Uke.

(5) Take a sliding step to the left into a right-footed Kokutsu-Dachi position executing a Morote-Uke.

(6) Look forwards again and prepare for a Morote-Uke.

(7) Take a sliding step to the rear into a left-footed Kokutsu-Dachi position executing a Morote-Uke.

(8) Go forward into a right-footed Zenkutsu-Dachi position with an Oi-Zuki.

(9) Remaining in the same position bend the right arm up similar to the position in a shortened version of the Uchi-Uke. As you do this the hips remain straight.

(10) Go forward into a left-footed Zenkutsu-Dachi position with an Oi-Zuki.

(11) Remaining in the same position bend the left arm up similar to the position in a shortened version of the Uchi-Uke. As you do this the hips remain straight.

(12) Go forward into a right-footed Zenkutsu-Dachi position with an Oi-Zuki. **KIAI.**

(13) Turn round on the spot slowly 180° to the rear preparing for a Gyaku-Tsukami-Uke. The right arm is pushed upwards as you do this and the left hand is closed round the wrist of the right hand.

(14) Slowly, the arms are brought back straight to the body for a Gyaku-Tsukami-Uke in a left-footed Zenkutsu-Dachi position.

(15) Execute a right-footed Mae-Geri kick and at the same time sharply bring both arms down to the sides of the body.

(16) Land well forward into a right-footed Kosa-Dachi position and pull back the right arm over the head for an Uraken-Uchi.

(17) Right-footed Kosa-Dachi doing an Uraken-Uchi.

(18) Push the left leg backwards quickly into a right-footed Zenkutsu-Dachi position doing an Uchi-Uke.

(19) Remaining in the same position do a Gyaku-Zuki.

(20) Remaining in the same position do an Oi-Zuki.

(21) Turn round on the spot 180° to the rear preparing for a left Gedan-Barai and a right Uchi-Uke.

(22) Left-footed Kokutsu-Dachi doing a left Gedan-Barai and a right Uchi-Uke.

(23) Slowly pull the left leg in and prepare for a left Gedan-Barai.

(24) Renoji-Dachi position doing a left Gedan-Barai.

(25) Slowly go forward into left-footed Zenkutsu-Dachi position preparing for a Gyaku-Tsukami-Uke. The right arm is pushed upwards as you do this and the left hand is closed round the wrist of the right hand.

(26) Slowly, the arms are brought back straight to the body for a Gyaku-Tsukami-Uke in a left-footed Zenkutsu-Dachi position.

(27) Execute a right-footed Mae-Geri kick and at the same time sharply bring both arms down to the sides of the body.

(28) Land well forward into a right-footed Kosa-Dachi position and pull back the right arm over the head for an Uraken-Uchi.

(29) Right-footed Kosa-Dachi doing an Uraken-Uchi.

(30) Push the left leg backwards quickly into a right-footed Zenkutsu-Dachi position doing an Uchi-Uke.

(31) Remaining in the same position do a Gyaku-Zuki.

(32) Remaining in the same position do an Oi-Zuki.

(33) Turn round on the spot 180º to the rear preparing for a left Gedan-Barai and a right Uchi-Uke.

(34) Left-footed Kokutsu-Dachi doing a left Gedan-Barai and a right Uchi-Uke.

(35) Slowly pull the left leg in and prepare for a left Gedan-Barai.

(36) Renoji-Dachi position doing a left Gedan-Barai.

(37) Look left and get ready for a Manji-Uke.

(38) Do a Manji-Uke in a left-footed Kokutsu-Dachi position.

(39) Remaining in the same position lay the fists one over the other on the right hip.

(40) Take a gliding step to the left into a Kiba-Dachi position with a Morote-Zuki. Both arms are stretched out.

(41) Front view.

(42) Look right and get ready for a Manji-Uke.

(43) Do a Manji-Uke in a right-footed Kokutsu-Dachi position.

(44) Remaining in the same position lay the fists one over the other on the left hip.

(45) Take a gliding step to the right into a Kiba-Dachi position with a Morote-Zuki. Both arms are stretched out.

(46) Bring the left leg under the middle of the centre of balance of your body and look 90º to the left. At the same time open the right hand and bring it up over the head similar to the movement in the Age-Uke.

(47) Front view.

(48) Glide forward slowly into a right-footed Kokutsu-Dachi with a Bo-Uke.

(49) Front view.

(50) Glide forward to do a Bo-Zuki.

(51) Front view.

(52) Jump round 360º preparing for a Shuto-Uke.

(53) Land in a right-footed Kokutsu-Dachi position doing a Shuto-Uke.

(54) Look left and lay the fists on the right hip, one over the other, and bring the left leg in.

(55) Do a left Yoko-Geri with a Uraken.

(56) Land into left-footed Zenkutsu-Dachi position doing a right Gyaku-Mae-Empi into the open left hand.

(57) Look right and lay the fists on the left hip, one over the other, and bring the right leg in.

(58) Do a right Yoko-Geri with a Uraken.

(59) Land into right-footed Zenkutsu-Dachi position doing a left Gyaku-Mae-Empi into the open right hand.

(60) Look 90º to the left and slowly go forward, changing into a left-footed Zenkutsu-Dachi position preparing for a Gyaku-Tsukami-Uke. The right arm is pushed upwards as you do this and the left hand is closed round the wrist of the right hand.

(61) Slowly, the arms are brought back straight to the body for a Gyaku-Tsukami-Uke in a left-footed Zenkutsu-Dachi position.

(62) Execute a right-footed Mae-Geri kick and at the same time sharply bring both arms down to the sides of the body.

(63) Land well forward into a right-footed Kosa-Dachi position and pull back the right arm over the head for an Uraken-Uchi.

(64) Right-footed Kosa-Dachi doing an Uraken-Uchi.

(65) Push the left leg backwards quickly into a right-footed Zenkutsu-Dachi position doing an Uchi-Uke.

(66) Remaining in the same position do a Gyaku-Zuki.

(67) Remaining in the same position do an Oi-Zuki.

(68) Look rearwards and slowly pull back preparing for an Haishu-Uke under the right arm. The upper body is bent forward slightly as you do this.

(69) Slowly execute the Haishu-Uke in a left-footed Zenkutsu-Dachi position. The hip is turned out and the upper body is leaning forward.

(70) Jump round 180º doing a right-footed Mikazuki-Geri into the open left hand.

(71) As you land do an Ushiro-Geri with the left foot. You are looking forwards and the hands are flat on the ground.

(72) Front view.

(73) Jump up, changing the feet over into left-footed Kokutsu-Dachi position and doing a Gedan-Shuto-Uke.

(74) Front view.

(75) Go forward into a right-footed Kokutsu-Dachi with a Shuto-Uke.

(76) Look rearwards over the left shoulder and turn through 270º on the right leg. At the same time prepare for a left Uchi-Uke.

(77) Left-footed Zenkutsu-Dachi doing an Uchi-Uke.

(78) Go forward into a Zenkutsu-Dachi position with an Oi-Zuki.

(79) Look 180º rearwards, bring the right leg together and prepare for a right Uchi-Uke.

(80) Right-footed Zenkutsu-Dachi position with an Uchi-Uke.

(81) Go forward into a left Zenkutsu-Dachi position with an Oi-Zuki. **KIAI.**

(82) Look 90º to the left and stand up into a Shizentai position.

Application for (10)-(11)

Application for (25)-(27)

Application for (37)-(40)

Application for (68)-(71)

2.5   Gankaku

Gankaku is an unusual Kata. The Kamae stance on one leg is not known in the other Kata, but is the prevalent characteristic of Gankaku. By using this stance, good balance can be learnt and this demands a high degree of stability. FUNAKOSHI gave the Kata its Japanese name *Gankaku*, which roughly translates as *crane on the rocks*. In so doing he wanted to remove the military aspect of the name of the originally Okinawan Kata *Chinto (Battle towards the East)* – still used in other styles, and 'Japanise' it.

Speaking about this Kata, NAKAYAMA says, "The name used for it now stems from the stances in it, which resemble those of a crane, sitting on a rock waiting to pounce on its prey. In this position one should have the feeling that you hamper and control the opponent's movements."

GANKAKU

Sequence of actions:

(1) Shizentai.

(2) Push the right leg backwards and at the same time prepare for a Sokumen-Awase-Uke. The open hands are pulled back to the right hip with the backs of the hands touching.

(3) Right leg back into a Kokutsu-Dachi position doing a Sokumen-Awase-Uke. The backs of the hands are touching. The left arm pushes the right one out.

(4) Snap the arms down onto the right hip, turning them as you do (as in the Heian Godan movement). The right elbow is pulled into the hip.

(5) Remaining in the same position do a left Tettsui-Uchi.

(6) Remaining in the same position do a Gyaku-Zuki.

(7) Look rearwards and turn round 180º on the left leg, at the same time lift up the right knee quickly and prepare to do a right-handed Gedan-Barai block.

(8) Side view of the movement.

(9) Place the foot down with a right-footed Fumikomi in a Kiba-Dachi position executing a right Gedan-Barai.

(10) Turn round to the rear 180º on the spot into a left Zenkutsu-Dachi with a Jodan-Juji-Uke. The hands are open and the right one is held over the left one.

(11) Remaining in the same position bring both arms slowly back to the body, closing the fists as you do.

(12) Jump up off the left leg and kick the right knee up into the air.

(13) Change over the legs.

(14) Execute a left Mae-Tobi-Geri.

(15) Land in a left-footed Zenkutsu-Dachi position with a Gedan-Juji-Uke.

(16) Look to the rear over the right shoulder. Turn round rearwards 180º on the right leg, at the same time get ready to do a Gedan-Juji-Uke from the right side of the body.

(17) Step forward into a left-footed Zenkutsu-Dachi position with a Gedan-Juji-Uke.

(18) Look rearwards and get ready on the spot to do a Gedan-Uke.

(19) Turn round 180º on the spot into a right Kokutsu-Dachi position with a Gedan-Barai. The left lower arm is held to the body with the back of the fist pointing towards the ground.

(20) Side view.

(21) Step forward into a left-footed Kokutsu-Dachi position with a Gedan-Shuto-Uke.

(22) Slowly take a step forwards into a right-footed Zenkutsu-Dachi position getting ready to do a Kakiwake-Uke hook with the open hands.

(23) Slowly go into a Zenkutsu-Dachi position delivering a Kakiwake-Uke.

(24) Look left 90º and slowly pull back ready for a Kakiwake-Uke.

(25) Slowly go left through 90º, and remaining in the same position, pull the left foot back into a Kiba-Dachi position delivering a Kakiwake-Uke – the backs of the hands are pointing towards the ground.

(26) Front view.

(27) Slowly move the left foot a little towards the right one, stand up and slowly bring both arms in a circle upwards in order to -

(28) - do a double Gedan-Barai. You are looking to the left.

(29) Sink down and get ready to do a Manji-Uke.

(30) Go forwards into a left-footed Kokutsu-Dachi position with a Manji-Uke.

(31) Place the right foot forwards a little, preparing for a Manji-Uke.

(32) Go forwards into a right-footed Kokutsu-Dachi position with a Manji-Uke.

(33) Look to the rear over the left shoulder. Turn round rearwards 180º on the right leg, at the same time get ready to do a Manji-Uke

(34) Go forwards into a left-footed Kokutsu-Dachi position with a Manji-Uke.

(35) Look 90º to the right. Pull the right leg in to the left one and place the fists onto the hip quickly, as in getting ready to do a Gedan-Juji-Uke.

(36) Kneel down on the right knee, holding the left knee bent. At the same time do a Gedan-Juji-Uke.

(37) Stand up and slowly push the right foot sideways into a Kiba-Dachi position. As you do, execute a slow double Uchi-Uke.

(38) Move the right foot in a little and slowly stand up, bringing both arms over the head in order to -

(39) - do a double Gedan-Barai.

(40) Place the arms akimbo, maintaining tension in them.

(41) Front view.

(42) Remaining on the spot execute a right elbow block position, turning the hips and changing over into a lesser version of the left-footed Zenkutsu-Dachi position.

(43) Execute a left elbow block position, again turning the hips and changing over into a lesser version of the right-footed Zenkutsu-Dachi position.

(44) Look to the rear over the right shoulder and, on the spot, turn round on the right leg. At the same time slowly bring the left foot in a little and get ready to do a double Uchi-Uke.

(45) Slowly turn round further into a right-footed Kiba-Dachi with a double Uchi-Uke.

(46) Look 90º left and slowly place your weight onto the right leg bringing the left leg into the hollow at the back of the right knee. Simultaneously get ready to do a Manji-Uke.

(47) The left foot is pinned into the back of the right knee. Bend the weight carrying leg slightly and slowly do a Manji-Uke.

(48) Sink down further on the leading leg and at the same time bring both fists on to the right hip, laying one over the other.

(49) Left Yoko-Geri with an Uraken-Uchi.

(50) Place the left leg down and immediately go forward into a right-footed Zenkutsu-Dachi position with an Oi-Zuki. **KIAI.**

(51) Slowly place your weight onto the rear leg bringing the right leg into the hollow at the back of the left knee. Simultaneously slowly get ready to do a Manji-Uke.

(52) The right foot is pinned into the back of the left knee. Bend the weight carrying leg slightly and slowly do a Manji-Uke.

(53) Sink down further on the leading leg and at the same time bring both fists on to the left hip, laying one over the other.

(54) Right Yoko-Geri with an Uraken-Uchi.

(55) Place the left leg down into a Kiba-Dachi position with a left Gyaku-Zuki.

(56) Look in the opposite direction. Slowly bring your weight over the right leg and the left leg is brought into the hollow at the back of the right knee. At the same time slowly prepare to do a Manji-Uke.

(57) The left foot is pinned into the back of the right knee. Bend the weight carrying leg slightly and slowly do a Manji-Uke.

(58) Sink down further on the leading leg and at the same time bring both fists on to the right hip, laying one over the other.

(59) Left Yoko-Geri with an Uraken-Uchi.

(60) Place the left leg down into a Kiba-Dachi position with a right Gyaku-Zuki.

(61) Front view.

(62) Get ready for a Jodan-Shuto-Uke.

(63) Change over into a right-footed Zenkutsu-Dachi position doing a Jodan-Shuto-Uke.

(64) Remaining in the same position do a left Tate-Empi-Uchi into the palm of the right hand.

(65) Remaining in the same position slap the right fist into the open left hand and quickly bring them to the left side of the body.

(66) Side view.

(67) Look to the rear over the right shoulder and shift the weight onto your right standing leg. Turn the palms of your hands over (as in the Heian Godan movement) and turn round clockwise 180º. The left foot is pinned into the back of the right knee.

(68) End the turning movement and lay the hands on to the right hip.

(69) The left fist is laid over the right one. The leg with the weight on is well bent and the left foot is pinned into the back of the right knee.

(70) Left Yoko-Geri with an Uraken-Uchi.

(71) Place the left leg down and immediately go forward into a right-footed Zenkutsu-Dachi position with an Oi-Zuki. **KIAI.**

(72) Front view.

(73) Look rearwards and slowly bring the left leg to the other for the -

(74) Shizentai.

Application for (2)-(6)

Application for (56)-(61)

Application for (43)-(45)

Applying sequence (63)-(64)

Applying sequence (67)-(69)

2.6   Chinte

Chinte still retains the original name given to this Kata. FUNAKOSHI wanted to rename it as *Shoin*, which, unlike numerous other renaming measures, did not go through. *Chinte* means literally *unusual hands*. An illustrative meaning – immediately obvious as this Kata contains numerous exceptional techniques with the hands, which are not found in any other Kata. Amongst these are, in particular, the Nihon-Nukite – a jab with two fingers into the eyes – and the Nakadaka-Ippon-Ken. NAKAYAMA recommends Chinte as a Kata for self-defence by women, since speed, skill and not very much body power are demanded in order to be greatly effective against an assailant.   As a competition bout, it is almost exclusively carried out by women. Not much is known about the origins of Chinte. One myth says that it stems from an Asiatic indigenous dance, which showed young women what they had to learn in order to survive in the world.

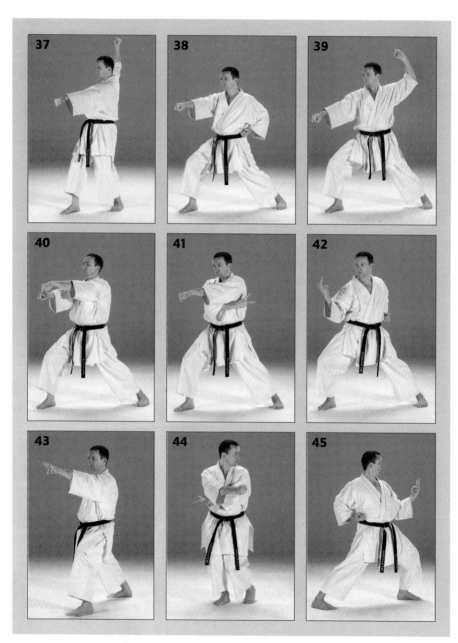

THE MASTER KATA

Sequence of actions:

(1) Shizentai.

(2) Slowly bring the feet together and lay the fists one over the other. The fist of the right hand is over the left hand one. At the same time look right.

(3) Slowly bring the right arm across and past the head for a -

(4) - Tettsui-Uchi. The left fist stays held to the body.

(5) Look left and once again lay the fists one over the other. This time the left fist is on top of the other one.

(6) Slowly bring the left arm across and past the head for a -

(7) - Tettsui-Uchi. The right fist stays held to the body.

(8) Open the hands and pull them in front of the body. At the same time switch the left foot forwards 90° into a -

(9) - Kiba-Dachi position executing a Jodan Morote-Shuto-Age-Uke. The thumbs and forefingers of both hands touch each other.

(10) Look right and changeover into a Fudo-Dachi position, getting ready to do right Tate-Shuto-Uke.

(11) Right-footed Fudo-Dachi with a Tate-Shuto-Uke.

(12) Stretch back the rear leg into a Zenkutsu-Dachi position. Turn the hip in and at the same time do a left Tate-Zuki into the open right hand.

(13) Slowly go forward into a left-footed Zenkutsu-Dachi position with a Tate-Shuto-Uke.

(14) Stretch back the rear leg into Zenkutsu-Dachi position. Turn the hip in and at the same time do a right Tate-Zuki into the open left hand.

(15) Slowly go forward into a right-footed Zenkutsu-Dachi position with a Tate-Shuto-Uke.

(16) Stretch back the rear leg into Zenkutsu-Dachi position. At the same time do a left Tate-Empi-Uchi into the palm of the right hand. **KIAI.**

(17) Front view.

(18) Look rearwards over the left shoulder and get ready to do a left Shuto-Uke on the spot.

(19) Left-footed Kokutsu-Dachi position doing a Shuto-Uke.

(20) Go forward into a right-footed Kokutsu-Dachi position doing a Shuto-Uke.

(21) Execute a left-footed Mae-Geri. The arms stay unchanged.

(22) Snap the foot back and at the same time get ready for a right Uchi-Uke double-block and a left Gedan-Barai.

(23) Place the foot down into a right-footed Zenkutsu-Dachi with a double block – right Uchi-Uke, left Gedan-Barai.

(24) Pull the rear leg in a little and at the same time bring the fist of the left hand onto the hip and stretch the right arm out.

(25) Bring the feet together and bring the right arm in a circle around the head, and -

(26) - up to the right, and –

(27) - then further downwards for a Gedan-Shuto-Uke. The right arm is slightly bent.

(28) Bring the right leg backwards a little and simultaneously both arms to the left. The hands are now open.

(29) Take the arms across the face to the right and in the same stance sink down lower.

(30) Glide to the right into a Kiba-Dachi position with a Gedan-Haito-Uke to the left.

(31) Look to the opposite side and in the same stance bring both arms in a circular motion upward to the left.

(32) Scribe a circle in a counter-clockwise direction with the arms and glide to the left into a Kiba-Dachi position with a Gedan-Haito-Uke to the right.

(33) Look forwards and remaining in the same position get ready for a double Uchi-Uke.

(34) Take a gliding step to the left and do a double Uchi-Uke.

(35) Put the right foot behind the left knee and slowly bring both arms up above the head in a crossed manner. The standing leg is bent.

(36) Slowly bring the arms down to the sides.

(37) Place the right foot forward a little and get ready to do a defensive strike down to the right – Nakadaka-Ippon-Ken.

(38) Place the foot down into a right-footed Zenkutsu-Dachi position and execute a right Nakadaka-Ippon-Ken.

(39) Remaining in the same position get ready to do a left Nakadaka-Ippon-Ken.

(40) Remaining in the same position execute a left Nakadaka-Ippon-Ken onto the right hand.

(41) Remaining in the same position get ready to do a right Nihon Nukite-Uchi-Uke.

(42) Remaining in the same position do a right Nihon Nukite-Uchi-Uke. The arms are held as in the Uchi-Uke.

(43) Go forward in a left-footed Zenkutsu-Dachi position with a Jodan Nihon-Nukite.

(44) Look rearwards over the left shoulder, pull the left leg up to the right one and prepare to do a left Nihon Nukite-Uchi-Uke.

(45) Turn round 180º to the rear and take a pace forwards for a Nihon Nukite-Uchi-Uke in a Zenkutsu-Dachi stance.

(46) Go forward into a right-footed Zenkutsu-Dachi position with Jodan Nihon-Nukite.

(47) Look 90º to the left and bring the forward leg in. Simultaneously prepare for a Teisho-Uke to the right.

(48) Go forwards 90° into a right-footed Fudo-Dachi with a Teisho-Uke.

(49) Remaining in the same position do a left Teisho-Uke.

(50) Front view.

(51) Bring the arms down to the rear quickly. The upper body is leaning slightly forward. You are continuing to look forwards.

(52) Turn round 180° on the spot to the rear, and -

(53) - do a Hasami-Zuki into a left-footed Fudo-Dachi. **KIAI.**

(54) Slowly take a pace forwards getting ready to do a Tate-Shuto-Uke.

(55) Carry on with the right Tate-Shuto-Uke into a Fudo-Dachi position.

(56) Stretch the rear leg into a Zenkutsu-Dachi position. Turn the hip in and at the same time do a left Tate-Zuki into the open right hand.

(57) Slowly take a pace forwards into left-footed Fudo-Dachi with a Tate-Shuto-Uke.

(58) Stretch the rear leg into a Zenkutsu-Dachi position. Turn the hip in and at the same time do a right Tate-Zuki into the open left hand.

(59) Pull the front leg backwards and jump to the rear. The arms are bent.

(60) Landing.

(61) Take another jump to the rear, but this time not so far as before.

(62) Landing.

(63) Take a last jump to the rear, each time make it less of a distance than before.

(64) Landing.

(65) Shizentai.

Application for (2)-(4)

Application for (9)

Application for (10)-(12)

Application for (15)-(16)

Application for (24)-(27)

Application for (29)-(30)

THE MASTER KATA

2.7 Unsu

The name *Unsu* literally means *hands in the clouds*. Unsu is the most spectacular Kata in Shotokan. The dynamic change of rhythm and the execution of a jumping movement 360° all make for suspense in and recognition of effort when doing a demonstration of this Kata and demands a high degree of control in this discipline. Unsu is also considered to be the most difficult of all the Shotokan Kata. This comes from the degree of difficulty of the jumping movements, which calls for a lot of athletic ability not seen, as a rule, in the other Kata. This is why training is mainly athletic for those who wish to use this one as a competition Kata. Unsu can also be found in the repertoire of the Shito-Ryu Kata. In that system the version taught is the older one and has a slower rhythm.

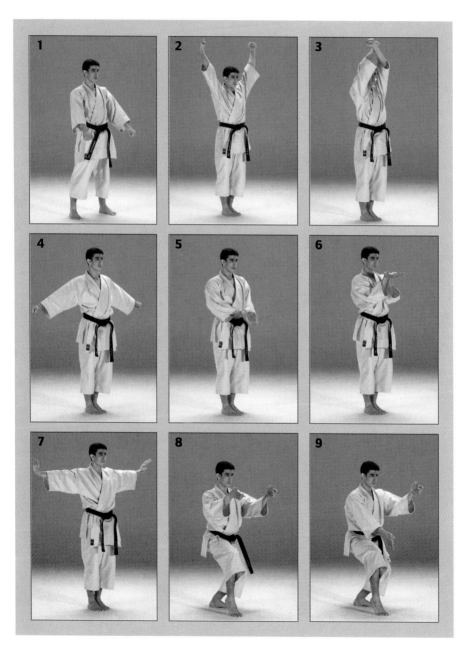

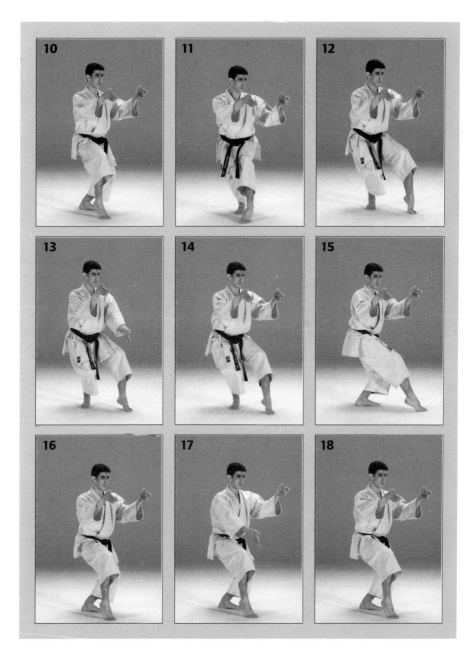

UNSU

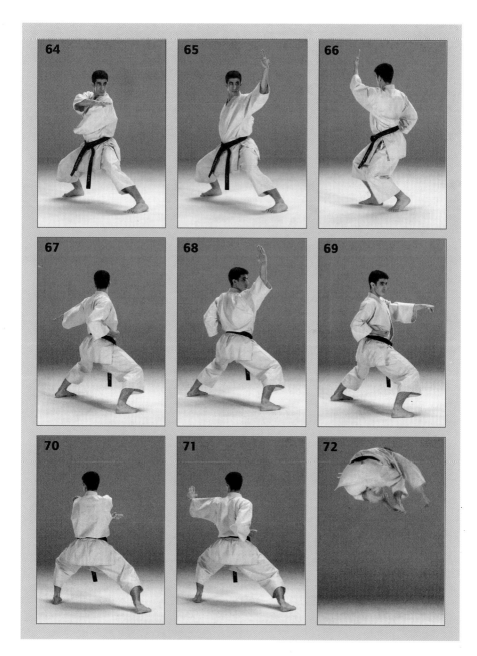

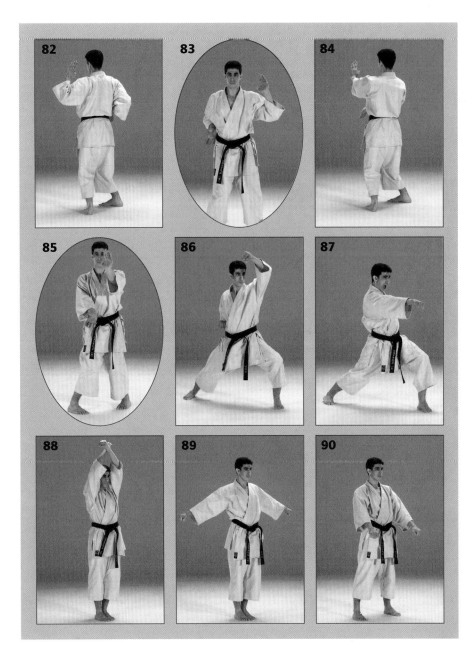

Sequence of actions:

(1) Shizentai.

(2) Bring the feet together and simultaneously, slowly raise both arms upwards -

(3) - over the head and then slowly -

(4) - bring them down to the sides.

(5) Slowly bring the edges of both hands – palms upwards – for a double Teisho-Uke at belt height.

(6) Slowly raise the hands up to the height of the chin and -

(7) - then slowly push both hands out to the sides with a Tate-Shuto-Uke.

(8) Go forward right into a Neko-Ashi-Dachi position and do a Keito-Uke with both hands. All the fingers, apart from the forefinger, are "folded back".

(9) Do a right-handed Gedan-Ippon-Nukite stabbing blow and immediately afterwards -

(10) - snap back into the same technique as before.

(11) Slowly go forward into a left-footed Neko-Ashi-Dachi position. At the same time the left foot is brought back in a semi-circle. The arm position remains unchanged.

(12) Left Neko-Ashi-Dachi with a double Keito-Uke.

(13) Stabbing left-handed blow Gedan-Ippon-Nukite and then immediately -

(14) - snap back into the same technique.

(15) Slowly go forward into a right-footed Neko-Ashi-Dachi position. At the same time the right foot is brought back in a semi-circle. The arm position remains unchanged.

(16) Right Neko-Ashi-Dachi with a double Keito-Uke.

(17) Stabbing right-handed blow Gedan-Ippon-Nukite and then immediately -

(18) - snap back into the same technique.

(19) 90º left into a left-footed Fudo-Dachi position with a Tate-Shuto-Uke.

(20) Remaining in the same position do a Gyaku-Zuki.

(21) Turn round rearwards 180º into a right-footed Fudo-Dachi with a Tate-Shuto-Uke.

(22) Remaining in the same position do a Gyaku-Zuki.

(23) 90º left into a left-footed Fudo-Dachi position with a Tate-Shuto-Uke.

(24) Remaining in the same position do a Gyaku-Zuki.

(25) Turn round rearwards 180º into a right-footed Fudo-Dachi with a Tate-Shuto-Uke.

(26) Remaining in the same position do a Gyaku-Zuki.

(27) Fall down to the right at 45º angle onto both hands. The right leg is lying angled under the body and the left leg is stretched out rearwards. Then immediately -

(28) - get ready to do a Mawashi-Geri with the left leg.

(29) Do a Mawashi-Geri against the opponent with the left leg.

(30) Roll over 90° onto the left side so that you are now lying on the left side of your body. The right leg is bent ready to deliver a Mawashi-Geri. Both hands lie flat on the ground.

(31) Do a Mawashi-Geri against the opponent with the right leg.

(32) The right leg is snapped back, at the same time looking right.

(33) Stand up to the right into a 45°-angle backwards (on to the start line). The feet are together with the knees well bent and the hands are brought upwards from below with a double Teisho-Uke (see Pictures 5 & 6).

(34) Slowly glide into a right-footed Kiba-Dachi position with a double Tate-Shuto-Uke. You continue to look to the right.

(35) Pull back the right leg and at the same time, with the left arm under the right one, get ready to -

(36) - do a left Keito-Uke and a right Teisho-Uke to the rear into a left-footed Zenkutsu-Dachi position. The hands are held as in an Ippon-Nukite.

(37) Pull back the left leg and at the same time, with the right arm under the left one, get ready to -

(38) - do a right Keito-Uke and a left Teisho-Uke to the rear into a right-footed Zenkutsu-Dachi position.

(39) Side view.

(40) Remaining in the same position do a left Haito-Uchi.

(41) Do a left Mae-Geri. The position of the arms remains unchanged. Snap back with a step and then -

(42) - turn round on the right standing leg 180° to the rear with a right Jodan-Soto-Uke. The left leg stays pulled in.

(43) Place the left leg back into a right-footed Zenkutsu-Dachi position with a Gyaku-Zuki.

(44) Turn round 180° on the spot with a right Haito-Uchi into a left-footed Zenkutsu-Dachi position.

(45) Do a right Mae-Geri. The position of the arms remains unchanged. Snap back with a step and then -

(46) - turn round on the left standing leg 180° to the rear with a left Jodan-Soto-Uke. The right leg stays pulled in.

(47) Place the right leg back into a right-footed Zenkutsu-Dachi position with a Gyaku-Zuki.

(48) Slowly bring the left leg in to the other to take up a Heisoku-Dachi position and at the same time bring both arms up into a cross over the head, and then -

(49) - bring them down to the sides. At the same time look 45° to the left.

(50) Slowly push the left leg forwards at an angle of 45°, simultaneously stretch the left arm upwards while the right remains unchanged. The left hand is open.

(51) Then slowly go forwards with the right leg. The arms changeover now, i.e., the right arm is held up on high. Get ready to -

(52) - do a right Gedan-Zuki in a right-footed Zenkutsu-Dachi position.

(53) Turn round 180° on the spot with a left Gedan-Zuki into a left-footed Zenkutsu-Dachi position.

(54) Turn round rearwards 180° on the spot with a right Gedan-Zuki into a right-footed Zenkutsu-Dachi position.

(55) Changeover the left foot pushing back 180° into a left-footed Fudo-Dachi position with a left Tate-Shuto-Uke.

(56) Get ready with the open right hand and -

(57) - bring the balls of the palms of the hands together for a Teisho-Hasami-Uke. As you do turn the hips in and stretch out the right leg into a Zenkutsu-Dachi position.

(58) Bring up the right knee between both arms and -

(59) - do a Mae-Geri-Kekomi with the heel. The arms are pulled in to the body. **KIAI.**

(60) Pull the right leg back again, pull back with the left arm, putting -

(61) - the leg down into Zenkutsu-Dachi position, do a right Oi-Zuki.

(62) Turn round 135° rearwards and get ready to do a Gedan-Barai with the right arm over the head.

(63) Go forward into a Kiba-Dachi position with a right Gedan-Barai. You are also looking to the right.

(64) Look left and remaining in the same position, with the left hand under the right one, get ready to -

(65) - do a Jodan-Haito-Uke.

(66) Look right again and bring the left hand past the head.

(67) Go forward into a Kiba-Dachi position with a left Shuto-Gedan-Barai.

(68) Look right and in the same position do a right Jodan-Haito-Uke.

(69) Remaining in the same position do a Gyaku-Zuki.

(70) Changeover to the left foot and slowly turn 180° into a left-footed Fudo-Dachi position and simultaneously get ready to do a Tate-Shuto-Uke with the left arm.

(71) Do a left-footed Fudo-Dachi (or a Kokutsu-Dachi) with a Tate-Shuto-Uke.

(72) Do a Mikazuki-Geri with the right foot into the open left hand, jump round 360°, at the same time bringing the knee as close to the body as possible.

(73) Land with a left Ushiro-Geri, the palms of the hands are flat on the ground and you are looking forward.

(74) Stand up, going forward into a Sanchin-Dachi position and slowly prepare for a Mawashi-Uke. Both hands are open. The left hand is at face height and the right hand is lower down at belly-button level.

(75) Front view.

(76) Pull both hands slowly to the body. The right hand is at head height and the left hand is at belt height. The hands have to be turned over.

(77) Front view.

(78) Push both arms out slowly.

(79) Front view.

(80) Go forward into a right-footed Sanchin-Dachi position and slowly prepare for a Mawashi-Uke. Both hands are open. The left hand is at face height and the right hand is lower down at belly-button level.

(81) Front view.

(82) Pull both hands slowly to the body. The left hand is at head height and the right hand is at belt height. The hands have to be turned over.

(83) Front view.

(84) Push both arms out slowly.

(85) Front view.

(86) Turn round rearwards 180° on the spot into a Zenkutsu-Dachi position with a left Age-Uke.

(87) Remaining in the same position do a Gyaku-Zuki. **KIAI.**

(88) Pull the front leg slowly back for a Heisoku-Dachi stance. At the same time cross both arms over above the head and -

(89) - slowly bring them down to the sides.

(90) Shizentai.

Application for (5)-(7)

Application for (8)-(10)

Application for (28)-(31)

Application for (33)-(47)

Application for (59)-(60)

WANKAN

2.8 Wankan

Why Wankan and Ji'in were never adopted into NAKAYAMA's standard work "Best Karate", although they belong to the 26 Shotokan Kata, is not quite clear. Was it intentional or was it that NAKAYAMA's sudden death in 1987 precluded this? What is certain, however, is that Wankan is one of the lesser-practised Kata in Shotokan.

Wankan is the shortest Kata in Shotokan. Characterised by the Jodan double-block Kakiwake-Uke when going forward, it is the only Kata in Shotokan with only one Kiai. Its origin is from the Tomari-Te of the Matsumura tradition. The name *Wankan* literally means the *King's crown* – possibly derived from the first three movements in the Kata. The third technique sequence resembles the middle part of a crown, which is set between two side diadems represented by the techniques embodied in the first two sequences.

THE MASTER KATA

THE MASTER KATA

Sequence of actions:

(1) Shizentai.

(2) Look 45º to the left and slowly go into left-footed Kokutsu-Dachi position with a Kakiwake-Uke.

(3) Look right and make a crossover step left in front of right. The arms stay on the same side.

(4) Slowly go forward 45º into right-footed Kokutsu-Dachi position with a Kakiwake-Uke.

(5) Look forward and at the same time pull up the right foot while bringing the lower arms together for a Hasami-Uke.

(6) Go forward to the right placing the foot down into a Zenkutsu-Dachi. The arm position remains unchanged in the Hasami-Uke position.

(7) Slowly take a pace forwards into a left-footed Zenkutsu-Dachi position. The arm position remains unchanged in the Hasami-Uke position.

(8) Slowly take a pace forwards into a right-footed Zenkutsu-Dachi position and at the same time prepare to do a Gyaku-Tate-Shuto-Uke under the right arm.

(9) Go forward right into a Zenkutsu-Dachi position with a left Tate-Shuto-Uke.

(10) Remaining in the same position do an Oi-Zuki.

(11) Remaining in the same position do a Gyaku-Zuki.

(12) Look left and turn through 90º to the left. Simultaneously pull the left leg in a little and prepare for a left Gedan Sukui-Uke and a right Gedan Teisho-Uchi.

(13) Left into a Neko-Ashi-Dachi position with a left Gedan Sukui-Uke and a right Gedan Teisho-Uchi.

(14) Slowly pull back for a left Gyaku Tate-Shuto-Uke.

(15) Go forward slowly into a right-footed Zenkutsu-Dachi position with a Gyaku Tate-Shuto-Uke.

(16) Remaining in the same position do an Oi-Zuki.

(17) Remaining in the same position do a Gyaku-Zuki.

(18) Look to the rear and turn round on the spot through 180º. Simultaneously prepare for a left Gedan Sukui-Uke and a right Gedan Teisho-Uchi.

(19) Left into a Neko-Ashi-Dachi position with a left Gedan Sukui-Uke and a right Gedan Teisho-Uchi.

(20) Slowly pull back for a left Gyaku Tate-Shuto-Uke.

(21) Go forward slowly right into a Zenkutsu-Dachi position with a Gyaku Tate-Shuto-Uke.

(22) Remaining in the same position do an Oi-Zuki.

(23) Remaining in the same position do a Gyaku-Zuki.

(24) Look right over the right shoulder. Pull the right foot back and pull back with the right arm under the left one.

(25) Go forward to the right into a Kiba-Dachi position with a Tettsui-Uchi.

(26) Execute a left-footed Mae-Geri.

(27) Place the foot down into a left Zenkutsu-Dachi position with an Oi-Zuki.

(28) Execute a right-footed Mae-Geri.

(29) Place the foot down into a right Zenkutsu-Dachi position with an Oi-Zuki.

(30) Execute a left-footed Mae-Geri.

(31) Place the foot down into a left Zenkutsu-Dachi position with an Oi-Zuki.

(32) Look over the right shoulder to the rear with both fists laid one on the other on the left hip.

(33) Turn round 180° on the spot into a right-footed Fudo-Dachi position with a Yama-Zuki. **KIAI.**

(34) Shizentai.

Application for (5)

Application for (12)-(17)

Application for (25)-(27)

Application for (33)

THE MASTER KATA

2.9   Ji'in

Like Wankan, this Kata belongs to those Shotokan Kata that have been rather neglected. Actually it could be called *Jion-Sho* because it contains many of the basic elements of Jion. However, it is longer and contains several techniques carried out in the same stance such as the final sequences with Uchi-Uke, Gedan-Barai and Jodan-Chudan Ren-Zuki. Otherwise the repertoire demanded in Ji'in consists of practically all simple, but effective basic techniques carried out from the Zenkutsu-Dachi and Kiba-Dachi stances. Its origin comes from the Tomari-Te. FUNAKOSHI wanted to rename it *Shokyo (The shade of the pine tree)*. A terminology, like many of his attempts at renaming, that didn't come about. The Japanese name of the *Ji'in Kata* means *Mercy* and *Friendliness*.

THE MASTER KATA

Sequence of actions:

(1) Shizentai.

(2) Slowly bring the feet together and lay the right fist into the left hand. The arms are bent (as in Jion).

(3) Go backwards to the left and at the same time prepare to do a right Gedan-Barai and a left Uchi-Uke.

(4) Go right into a Zenkutsu-Dachi position with a double-block left Uchi-Uke and right Gedan-Barai.

(5) Look left and prepare for a Manji-Uke.

(6) Left Kokutsu-Dachi with a Manji-Uke.

(7) Look to the other side and turning on the spot through 180º prepare for a Manji-Uke.

(8) Go right into Kokutsu-Dachi with a Manji-Uke.

(9) Look 135º to the left, bring in the left leg and prepare for an Age-Uke.

(10) Go forward 45º into a left-footed Zenkutsu-Dachi position with an Age-Uke.

(11) Go forward into a right-footed Zenkutsu-Dachi position with an Oi-Zuki.

(12) Look and turn 90º to the right preparing for an Age-Uke. At the same time the right leg is brought in to the left one.

(13) Go forward into a right-footed Zenkutsu-Dachi position with an Age-Uke.

(14) Go forward into a left-footed Zenkutsu-Dachi position with an Oi-Zuki.

(15) Look 45º to the left and place the left foot forwards preparing for a Gedan-Barai.

(16) Go forward into a left-footed Zenkutsu-Dachi position with a Gedan-Barai.

(17) Take a step forward preparing to do a right Shuto-Uchi.

(18) Place the foot down into Kiba-Dachi position with a right Shuto-Uchi.

(19) Take a step forwards into a Kiba-Dachi with a left Shuto-Uchi.

(20) Take another step forwards into a Kiba-Dachi position with a right Shuto-Uchi. **KIAI.**

(21) Angle the left leg 45º to the left and slowly turn round rearwards on the spot with a Kakiwake-Uke into a left-footed Zenkutsu-Dachi.

(22) Do a right-legged Mae-Geri. The arms remain unchanged.

(23) Place the foot down into a right-footed Zenkutsu-Dachi with an Oi-Zuki.

(24) Remaining in the same position do a Gyaku-Zuki.

(25) Remaining in the same position do a double-block, right Gedan-Barai and a left Uchi-Uke.

(26) Look 90º to the right and slowly change into an angled turn 90º to the right with a Kakiwake-Uke into a right-footed Zenkutsu-Dachi.

(27) Do a left-legged Mae-Geri. The arms remain unchanged

(28) Place the foot down into a left-footed Zenkutsu-Dachi with an Oi-Zuki.

(29) Remaining in the same position do a Gyaku-Zuki.

(30) Remaining in the same position do a double-block, left Gedan-Barai and a right Uchi-Uke (the way to carry out the techniques in Sequences 26-30 is the same as those in Sequences 21-25 – only on the other side).

(31) Look over the right shoulder. Pull the right foot in to the left one. Turn round from the back 315° and at the same time prepare to do a Tettsui-Uchi.

(32) Go forward into a right-footed Kiba-Dachi with a Tettsui-Uchi.

(33) Turn round from the rear and prepare to do a left Tettsui-Uchi.

(34) Go forward into a Kiba-Dachi with a Tettsui-Uchi.

(35) Take a pace forwards and prepare for a right Tettsui-Uchi.

(36) Go forward right into a Kiba-Dachi with a Tettsui-Uchi.

(37) Slowly take a pace forwards at an angle of 45° and prepare for Tate-Shuto-Uke.

(38) Slowly continue into a left-footed Zenkutsu-Dachi position with a Tate-Shuto-Uke.

(39) Remaining in the same position do a Gyaku-Zuki.

(40) Remaining in the same position do an Oi-Zuki.

(41) Do a right-legged Mae-Geri.

(42) Place the foot down to the rear from the Mae-Geri at the same time doing a right Gyaku-Zuki.

(43) Remaining in the same position do a double-block, right Uchi-Uke and left Gedan-Barai.

(44) Look over the left shoulder rearwards and pull in the left foot. At the same time turn through an angle of 225° on the right leg preparing for a double-block.

(45) Place the left foot out sideways into a Kiba-Dachi position with a double-block, left Uchi-Uke and right Gedan-Barai.

(46) Remaining in the same position bring the left arm downwards, without any preparation in between, for a Gedan-Barai. The right arm remains unchanged.

(47) Remaining in the same position do a double-block Uchi-Uke.

(48) Remaining in the same position do a left Jodan-Zuki.

(49) Remaining in the same position do a right Chudan-Zuki. **KIAI.**

(50) Slowly bring the feet together and lay the right fist into the left hand.

(51) Shizentai.

Application for (18)

Application for (21)-(22)

Application for (37)-(43)

3 Karate Stances

The Kata include all the Karate stance positions. They make it possible to fight from short, middle and long distances. Therefore, at this juncture, here is a short set of illustrations depicting the Karate stance positions.

3.1 Heisoku-Dachi 3.2 Musubi-Dachi 3.3 Heiko-Dachi

3.4 Hachiji-Dachi 3.5 Zenkutsu-Dachi 3.6 Kokutsu-Dachi

3.7 Kiba-Dachi 3.8 Neko-Achi-Dachi 3.9 Sanchin-Dachi

3.10 Fudo-Dachi 3.11 Kosa-Dachi 3.12 Renoji-Dachi

4 Recurring Techniques in the Kata

At this point we have the opportunity to have a look at some of the recurring techniques that often appear in the Shotokan Kata – by phases and in detail. It is worth paying attention to the starting position, the movement(s) in-between and the correct final position of these techniques. These should be practised intensively in order to avoid mistakes.

4.1 Manji-Uke

4.2 Yoko-Geri, Uraken, Empi

4.3 Kakiwake-Uke

4.4 Tate-Shuto-Uke

4.5 Haishu-Uke

4.6 Morote-Uke

4.7 Fumikomi

5 Appendix

5.1 Bibliography

CROFT, A.: Shotokan Karate. Ramsbury 2001.

ENOEDA, K.: Shotokan Karate Advanced Kata Vol. 1-3. Norwich 1983-86.

ENOEDA, K.: Shotokan Karate 10th Kyu to 6th Kyu. London 1996.

ENOEDA, K.: Shotokan Karate 5th Kyu to Black Belt. London 1996.

FUNAKOSHI, G.: Karate-do Kyohan. Tokio 1978.

GRUPP, J.: Shotokan Karate. Kihon-Kumite-Kata. Oxford 2002.

GRUPP, J.: Shotokan Karate KATA Vol. 1. Oxford 2002.

GURSHARAN, S.: Advanced Shotokan Karate Handbook. Bedford 1997.

HABERSETZER, R.: Shotokan Kata, Karate-Do Tome 1. Paris 1992.

HASSELL, R.G.: Shotokan Karate: Its History and Evolution. St. Louis 1998.

HEALY, K.: A Step-by-step Guide to Shotokan Karate. London 2000.

MILON, M.: Apprenez vos Katas de Base du Karaté Shotokan. Paris 1997.

NAKAYAMA, M.: Karate-Do. Dynamic Karate. Sprendlingen 1972.

NAKAYAMA, M.: Best Karate. Band 9-11. Tokio, New York, London 1989.

NISHIJAMA, H. & BROWN, R. C., Karate. Lauda 2001.

REILLY, R.L.: Complete Shotokan Karate. Boston 1998.

REILLY, R.L.: The Secrets of Shotokan Karate. Boston 2000.

SCHLATT: Shotokan No Hyakkajiten. Lauda 1995.

SCHMEISSER, E.: Bunkai. Secrets of Karate Kata, Volume 1: The Tekki Series. Missouri 2000.

SUGIYAMA, S.: 25 Shoto-Kan Kata. Chicago 2000.

TRIMBLE, A. & MORRIS, V.: Karate Kata Applications. London 1995.

V. WEENEN, J.: Advanced Shotokan Karate Kata. Wollaston 1987.

WICHMANN, W.D.: Kata 1-3. Niedernhausen 1985, 1986, 1990.

WORLD KARATE FEDERATION, WKF: Karatedo Kata Model, Shiteikata. Tokio 2001.

APPENDIX

5.2 Photo & Illustration Credits

Photos: Christian Fritsch, FTB-Werbefotografie, Berlin
Cover design: Birgit Engelen, Stolberg

Contact with the Author

Questions about the book or queries about courses can be sent to the author at joachimgrupp@web.de.